12 DAYS OF
CHRISTMAS STORIES

PHIL CALLAWAY

CONTENTS

TELL US A STORY

Each year I promised I wouldn't be that guy. The one running around stores in a frenzy grabbing leftover gifts from vacant shelves while "Silent Night" plays through tinny speakers. But there I was again, standing at the checkout, exhausted. "Did you find everything you were looking for?" the tired clerk asked me. "I didn't find my wife," I said. "Can you help me?" Laughter relieved the stress, but every Christmas I grew increasingly weary of the make-everyone-happy-shop-til-you-drop-last-minute-gift-buying panic attack.

And then grandchildren arrived. Perspective too. They love toys and chocolate and things that go "Bang!" But each Christmas Eve, they ask, "Bumpa, tell us a story." The storybooks we had were too long, so I dusted off some stories of my own and made others up. Some were a little goofy, others might coax a tear. Stories from the past and the present. Stories of the hope to come. No Christmas is quite complete at our house without this collection you hold in your hand.

Our grandkids are too many to fit on my lap now so my children help out. The only light comes from our Christmas tree, so I squint as I read and we huddle together, giggle and smile as the three-year-old drifts off to sleep. I hope these stories brighten my favourite season for you too.

From our house to yours, a very merry Christmas!

Phil Callaway

CHAPTER 1

GRANDPA'S GREATEST GIFT

"Our hearts grow tender with childhood memories and love of kindred, and we are better throughout the year for having, in spirit, become a child again at Christmastime."
– Laura Ingalls Wilder

Soft voices wake me this cold December morning. "Is it time yet, Dad?" Outside our darkened window a white quilt blankets the ground. Inside, three excited children are pulling at my covers: "Come on, Dad."

Oh yes. It's Christmas day. It's also ridiculously early. "Hey, go back to bed," I say. "It's September."

Down the hall we go, coming to a halt before five stockings, concealing forbidden treasures.

"What about we eat 'em?" Jeffrey is three and speaks for the others.

"Not yet," I reply. "Wait 'til Mommy wakes up. Ssshhh."

We plug in the Christmas tree lights, then sit quietly on the couch as I tell them a tale from my childhood. A tale of Christmas past...

Once a year we children searched the skies for Grandpa. He always touched down during the Christmas season, so we would wait in the airport, our noses pressed against the frozen glass in painful anticipation.

I loved Grandpa. For one thing, he was the only one I knew who drank cough syrup straight from the bottle, oblivious to its high alcoholic content. And his bald head was as smooth as polished brass—only it grew less hair. I think the barber merely glued a stainless steel bowl to his head one day and said, "That will be $1.50."

We loved Grandpa for his size too. He was…well…a big man, poundage-wise. Grandpa Callaway could never be found far from a box of chocolates and the years had charged him for it. There were definite advantages to Grandpa's girth, however. It was perfect to hide behind during Hide and Seek, and when he laughed—which was often—he put his whole body into it. Perhaps best of all, the five of us found room on Grandpa's lap to hear the Christmas story year after year.

Most importantly, Grandpa always brought a gallon of genuine maple syrup and a brown leather suitcase heavy with brightly-wrapped packages (mostly for my sister).

But this Christmas, it looked like Grandpa's plane had arrived without him. Other grandpas arrived to the hugs and kisses of kids like us. But not Grandpa Callaway.

Then Dad noticed someone off to one side. Could it be? He was the right size. He had the right face. But he also had hair.

"What in the wor—?" said Dad.

"A wig—" replied Mom. "Sort of."

Moments later a restroom mirror told Grandpa why he'd escaped our notice. The wig was on sideways, the Made in Canada tag sloping neatly over his left ear. "Oh say," said Grandpa. "Oh say."

But the news would not get better. Grandpa's luggage, it seemed, had not made the journey with him. "OH SSSAY!" said Grandpa, through his false teeth.

And I began to piece the implications together. No maple syrup. No brightly-wrapped presents. And then the strangest thing happened. I realized it didn't matter.

Christmas would come without maple syrup and presents. Games would be played. Songs sung. Stories told. You see, Grandpa had brought us the best gift of all: himself.

Of course, Grandpa wasn't taking it quite so well. As we climbed into the car, I heard him mutter, "Oh say!" Then he reached for the cough syrup.

"Didn't you get anything at all?" asks Stephen.

"Yes, we did. But I don't remember the presents. I just remember Grandpa."

"Did he tell any stories?"

"Oh yes. He especially loved to read the Christmas story—of the Light that came blazing into the world. Of the Son of God, in a barn. And he told us that God could have given us anything He wanted. But He gave us the best gift of all: Himself."

Above us, suspended from a red string is a row of Christmas cards. In the center hangs my favourite: "If our greatest need had been information, God would have sent us an educator. But our greatest need was forgiveness, so God sent us a Saviour!"

In the soft glow of the Christmas tree, Rachael and Stephen sit in wonder. "Tell it again, Daddy," they say. "Tell it again."

Jeffrey sits quietly, looking at the stockings, and wondering about something else. "What about we eat 'em?" he says.

"Christmas is like candy; it slowly melts in your mouth sweetening every taste bud, making you wish it could last forever."
-Richelle E. Goodrich

The Story of Christmas Reflection

The goosebumps of Christmas morning make it hard to wait. Whether you are 3 or 63, enduring the weeks before Christmas stretches our patience. Some wait for presents to be unwrapped. Others wait for loved ones to arrive. But we all must learn to hold on.

The first Christmas was an experience of waiting. God promised to send the Messiah, and though the delay was long, God's promises never fail. Simeon knew that. Luke records that Simeon was told by God he would live to see the Messiah. So this righteous man greeted every sunrise with, "Maybe this is the day!" Simeon didn't have a calendar to count down to Christmas. He had to have open eyes and firm hope daily. When Mary and Joseph brought Jesus into the Temple, the Spirit whispered to Simeon, "This is the One!" This devout man burst into prayer and praise. His wait was over! Our wait is over as well. Jesus has come as light to our darkness and life to our death. The gift of God has arrived. In truth today, we are not waiting for presents, family or feast. While we wait for Christmas, we are waiting for Christ.

 ### Read Simeon's story from Luke 2:25-32

"Now there was a man in Jerusalem called Simeon, who was righteous and devout. He was waiting for the consolation of Israel, and the Holy Spirit was on him. It had been revealed to him by the Holy Spirit that he would not die before he had seen the Lord's Messiah. Moved by the Spirit, he went into the temple courts. When the parents brought in the child Jesus to do for him what the custom of the Law required, Simeon took him in his arms and praised God, saying:

'Sovereign Lord, as you have promised, you may now dismiss your servant in peace. For my eyes have seen your salvation, which you have prepared in the sight of all nations: a light for revelation to the Gentiles, and the glory of your people Israel.'"

Let Phil tell the story!

Scan the QR code with your smart phone or tablet to go directly to a video of Phil Callaway sharing the story in this chapter. Watch with the whole family!

scan this code!

CHAPTER 2

WHITE CHRISTMAS

"My idea of Christmas, whether old-fashioned or modern, is very simple: loving others. Come to think of it, why do we have to wait for Christmas to do that?"
–Bob Hope

What is the bestselling Christmas song of all time? No, it isn't "Grandma Got Run Over by a Reindeer." It's "White Christmas" by Bing Crosby. In fact, "White Christmas" is the best-selling single of all time, with estimated sales of more than 50 million copies.

Our Laugh Again program is broadcast in southern latitudes like Curacao, where a white Christmas is nothing more than a dream, a postcard. Listeners there would love to experience a white Christmas, a flurry of soft white flakes landing upon their tongues and melting. Hot chocolate sipped by a warm fire while they thaw out their frost-bitten toes.

Be warned. Snow is not all Hollywood cracks it up to be. It's cold. It's wet. It's slippery. It gets in your boots and in your ears. If you fall in a snow drift after your mother has dressed you in forty pounds of parkas and scarves and mittens, you will not stand up without the help of other third-grade classmates. Snow covers your car, your driveway, your sidewalk, and when you remove it with a shovel time after time, you will think to yourself, this is a lot like cleaning the house with toddlers around.

When I was a kid, I loved snow. Snow meant snow forts, snowballs, snowmen, and plunging down steep hills on rickety toboggans headed straight for a tree. Being the youngest, I often found myself beneath piles of it with my brothers perched on top. If my sister didn't dig me out, I might still be there. I loved every minute of it, of course. I loved getting

even with my brothers by carefully releasing a hard-packed snowball straight at them, then running like the wind.

But snow began to lose its appeal for me as I got older. It became inconvenient. Uncomfortable. When that first November…or October…or August blizzard hit, I moaned, groaned, whimpered and grabbed the shovel. I saw the white stuff, and thought of green stuff. Like grass and palm trees. I fired up my search engine and scoured the web for cheap flights to the tropics.

And then, Milton arrived from Uganda. He came to stay with my son Steve. Milton had heard of snow, but hadn't seen it. The day after he arrived in Canada, the cold stuff left the dark clouds above and descended; landing softly all around him like his mother was tucking him in with a soft blanket of white. I mourned the loss of summer. Milton didn't. He danced and giggled and cheered. He frolicked in the snow like a giddy school kid. Milton built his very first snowman, tasted his very first snowflake.

"I am so blessed to see this," he said. "I love snow! It's my favourite thing." We shivering Canadians looked at him as if he needed to search for his marbles. Milton didn't mind. Like the laughing children around him, he was having too much fun.

"God loves me so much," he said. "He let me see snow."

So contagious was Milton's joy, that I found myself grinning and thanking God that Milton got to see the snow. I found myself asking why I'd lost the joy of childhood, wondering why I'd lost the wonder.

When I was a kid, snow meant ice hockey and snow forts and careening down hills on truck inner tubes. Then it came to mean cold and shoveling and frozen appendages. Milton helped me reconsider a verse in Isaiah 1. A verse that talks of snow and the wonder of God's mercy.

"Come, let's talk this over! says the Lord. No matter how deep the stain of your sins, I can take it out and make you as clean as freshly fallen snow. Even if you are stained as red as crimson, I can make you white as wool!"

My friend Milton is back in Uganda now, where he sometimes listens to Laugh Again.

If you're reading this, Milton, thanks for reminding me of the wonder of God's grace and mercy. I hope you enjoy those warm winter nights in your country. And, in honour of you, I think I'll put on forty pounds of clothing, go outside, and build a snowman.

"I wish we could put up some of the Christmas spirit in jars and open a jar of it every month."
– Harlan Miller

The Story of Christmas Reflection

We take for granted what is common to us. When you've seen snow (perhaps too much of it!) the marvel of snowflakes and beauty of white-shrouded hills is ignored. We fail to appreciate what is at our feet.

When Jesus was born, He was largely ignored. When He was laid in a manger, most of Bethlehem slept. Jerusalem was too busy to note this young Boy presented in the Temple. In his Gospel, John tells us that Jesus came and was unrecognized in this world. He was simply "another child, a carpenter in a small town, a preacher on dusty roads." But Jesus is more. He is the Light of the world, God in the flesh, filled with grace and truth. He extends to us one blessing after another!

Perhaps we can become immune to the wonders of Jesus. We've heard the story so many times. We've read the Bible, so many verses. Cold hearts can be numbed to the beauty of Christ. If that rings true for you this Christmas, ask God for the gift of open eyes. To see afresh like Milton and proclaim, "I am so blessed to see this!" May God grant us joyful hearts, like children giggling as they make angels in the snow.

Read the Mystery of Jesus Coming from John 1:10-14

"He was in the world, and though the world was made through him, the world did not recognize him. He came to that which was his own, but his own did not receive him. Yet to all who did receive him, to those who believed in his name, he gave the right to become children of God—children born not of natural descent, nor of human decision or a husband's will, but born of God.

The Word became flesh and made his dwelling among us. We have seen his glory, the glory of the one and only Son, who came from the Father, full of grace and truth."

CHAPTER 3

THE LAST CHRISTMAS GIFT

"The worst gift is a fruitcake. There is only one fruitcake in the entire world, and people keep sending it to each other."
–Johnny Carson

The older I get, the more I'm convinced that memory and smell are linked. I love the smell of Christmas: Sugar cookies baking. Fireplace crackling. Burnt turkey sizzling. I love the taste of Christmas too: Smashed potatoes. Mandarin oranges. Buttered yams. Fresh dirt from one of my brother Tim's incoming snowballs. Ah, Christmastime.

When I was a child of eight or nine and Christmas was barely a week away, I sinned greatly. Each year my grandfather came to visit. And that year, I sneaked into his room while he was snoring, reached past a cup of water that held his false teeth, which I think were still moving, stole an entire box of chocolates, locked myself in the bathroom and ate both layers. I can still taste that chocolate. I can still feel that strap. Few spankings were worth it. This was one of them. It made me wonder if sometimes you're almost better off asking for forgiveness than permission.

Each December morning, my sister Ruth and I would wrap ourselves in a blanket, and sit on a toasty warm living room heat vent, coveting toys from the Sears catalog. Just behind our head was an electrical outlet. December was so cold in those days that frost had crawled right through the wall and out of that outlet. Next to it was a steel doorknob. The previous afternoon my brother Tim said, "Lick it." I said, "Why?" He said, "Because it's interesting. And you want to do interesting things if you're going to live an interesting life." I said, "What does it taste like?" He said, "Remember the battery you licked last summer? This is bigger. You'll not forget it." Then he pulled a shiny quarter from his pocket. "I'll give you this." A quarter! It would buy more candy than a kid could eat. So I opened my mouth and slapped my tongue on that doorknob. It stayed there. I said, "Help. Help." Tim grabbed a pitcher of water and dumped it on my head. He's a Baptist minister now. He was practicing. And he was right. I never forgot that doorknob.

Otherwise, I was a reasonably bright chap. My sister pointed to certain toys. "What do they do?" she asked. If I didn't know, I made stuff up. "That doll's head wobbles side to side, then just pops right off." "Woah," she said. She was so impressed at my knowledge. I was too.

One page held a dream for me. It was a yellow-handled bow with real suction-cup arrows. "If only I could pull the wrapping off that," I told my sister, "my Christmas would be perfect." She shook her head. When I told my brother, he said, "You kidding? After what you did to Grandpa's chocolates? You'll be lucky to get a hand-me-down toothbrush."

Still I showed the bow and arrow to my dad. "$10.99!" he winced. "You wanna put us in the Poor House?" I wasn't sure. I was willing. I wondered what the Poor House would look like. What would we do there? Would Grandpa visit? Would he bring chocolates?

As December 25th drew near, I scanned the growing pile beneath the tree. Nothing. A shiny green package near the back was the right size, so late one night while everyone was sleeping, I shook it and looked at the nametag. "Ruth." It was my sister's. Most of them seemed to be hers. I squeezed the ones that said "Philip." They felt like practical gifts: socks, deodorant, underwear. Things you don't tell your friends about on Boxing Day.

The worst thing about Christmas morning was the waiting. My parents made us eat breakfast first. Then we did the dishes. And swept the floor. And vacuumed. And washed the walls, I

music. For my mom. The second was a box of chocolates for my grandpa. From me. Though I only put a quarter into buying it. The last gift was green and shiny and just the right size. My sister grinned. And picked it up. And sat beside me, taunting me. Turning it over and over.

Then the most unexpected thing in history happened: she turned and handed it to me. "Open it," she said. "It's yours. Tim put my name on it to fool you."

Mom wanted me to save the wrapping paper for next year. It was too late. I let out a Whoop! And danced around holding the bow and arrow high like the Stanley Cup. Grandpa stopped sampling chocolates and smiled widely.

"You be careful with that, Son," said Mom.

"He'll be fine," said Dad.

I remember only a handful of gifts from my childhood. A Detroit Red Wings hockey jersey. A Hot Wheels race-car set. I remember ice-skating and carol-singing, and the story of a Baby whose tiny brow was made for thorns; whose blood would one day cleanse the world. But it was the last gift that made Christmas come alive for me. That bow and arrow made me realize that Christmas is all about grace. A gift I don't deserve coming along when I least expect it. Changing everything. Forever.

"For unto us a child is born, unto us a son is given…they shall call His name Immanuel, God with us…And He shall save His people from their sins."

A child of eight or nine doesn't think of these things. I only knew that I couldn't wait to try that gift out. I wolfed down turkey and my Mom's special dressing and fruitcake so thick you could hear it hit bottom. And I tip-toed after my brother as he headed down the hallway that afternoon. I locked an arrow in place, took careful aim, pulled on the string and yelled, "Hey Tim! Merry Christmas!"

And I wondered just for a moment if I should ask permission or forgiveness.

think. Next we gathered in the living room and memorized the Gospel of Luke. In German. Low German and High German. Then Dad prayed for the troops in Vietnam and Korea and Russia and Saskatchewan, and missionaries in countries I couldn't pronounce.

Finally the time came. And this year the disappointment was overwhelming. With only three presents left beneath the tree, I held in my lap a small Tonka truck, a shirt with pins in it, and a cowboy poster that read, "When you reach the end of your rope, tie a knot in it and hang on."

The first remaining gift was a record album of old people's

"Never worry about the size of your Christmas tree. In the eyes of children, they are all 30 feet tall."
-Larry Wilde

The Story of Christmas Reflection

A song on the radio warns us every Christmas, "you better watch out, you better not cry!" It cautions us to, "be good for goodness sake!" The song is a threat to the naughty and applause for those who are nice. But is it true? If we think good things come only to those who are good, consider this:

Elizabeth and Zachariah were good, but the thing they wanted hadn't happened. Their prayers for a child went unanswered for decades. Now that the time for a baby had passed, they assumed it would never happen. Perhaps they wondered if their names were on the "naughty" list of Heaven. So when Gabriel told Zachariah that Elizabeth would have a child, he found it hard to believe. In fact, he argued that it couldn't happen. The angel told him to be quiet and stay that way for nine months! When the angel's words came true with a baby boy, Zachariah's mouth burst open to name him, "John!" John would be the announcer of the coming Messiah.

Despite the delay and Zachariah's disbelief, good things came to this couple. Not because they were always good— but because God is. Like a boy who found what he wanted under the tree despite eating all the chocolates, Christmas is not about gifts for the good, but grace for all.

Read Zachariah and Elizabeth's story from Luke 1:11-17

"Then an angel of the Lord appeared to him, standing at the right side of the altar of incense. When Zechariah saw him, he was startled and was gripped with fear. But the angel said to him: 'Do not be afraid, Zechariah; your prayer has been heard. Your wife Elizabeth will bear you a son, and you are to call him John. He will be a joy and delight to you, and many will rejoice because of his birth, for he will be great in the sight of the Lord. He is never to take wine or other fermented drink, and he will be filled with the Holy Spirit even before he is born. He will bring back many of the people of Israel to the Lord their God. And he will go on before the Lord, in the spirit and power of Elijah, to turn the hearts of the parents to their children and the disobedient to the wisdom of the righteous—to make ready a people prepared for the Lord.'"

Let Phil tell the story!

Scan the QR code with your smart phone or tablet to go directly to a video of Phil Callaway sharing the story in this chapter. Watch with the whole family!

scan this code!

CHAPTER 4

DANNY BROWN'S FIRST CHRISTMAS

"I loved Christmas when I was small. I'd pounce on my dad about five in the morning. He'd say, 'Hey, go back to bed! It's October!'"
–Phil Callaway

Christmases of my childhood were magical times, and few things were more magical than the Christmas program, a time when kids sang badly to great applause and sometimes raucous laughter, especially when they got mixed up and with giant cards spelled out "Christmas Rats," instead of Christmas star. The climax was, of course, the end of the program when we each received a sacred candy bag.

Danny Brown took up residence in the desk behind me one year, and in early December, his father forbade Danny from taking part in the program. Some said Mr. Brown was a real live atheist who was protesting a season gone mad with carols and mention of the Almighty.

So each Friday when we practiced, Danny sat in the balcony of our church. I pitied him. He would miss Sunday night's performance. And, worse, the coveted candy bags.

"Fairy tales," said Danny, when talking of Christmas. "A buncha clowns looking for an excuse to make more money." The only Christmas song he knew was one his father made up: "O Come Let Us Ignore Him."

Miss Thomas, our choir director, was a large woman. Her arms weighed more than two of me and she got quite a workout directing us. Those arms danced and shook and we loved her for it. Some adult made the mistake of stapling holly to the wall behind us, framing the edges of a huge banner that read "What Child Is This?" Now holly has rather sharp thorns if you leave it to dry and when we stood to sing, I eased a thorny clipping onto Beth Freeman's chair and when we sat down, she lived to rise again. "OW OW OW!" She howled. "Why you little—" she whirled and pointed at me. "Go to the balcony…NOW!" Miss Thomas ordered me.

I'd been there before. Danny was waiting there. As the children sang about angels and shepherds, I told Danny another version:

> While shepherds washed their socks by night,
> All seated on the ground
> The angel of the Lord came down
> And passed the soap around.
> And passed the soap around.

Ironically, my mother washed my mouth out with soap when I sang it for her. Danny, however, found it funnier than I expected, so I treated him to another:

> We three kings of Orient are
> Smoking on a rubber cigar.
> It was loaded, it exploded
> Now we're on yonder star.

A volcanic laugh built within the poor boy and he let out a loud yelp. Miss Thomas glared at us and brought her arms to a wobbly halt. "I've had about enough!" she yelled.

That's when I said to Danny something I still feel guilty for. "Then stop eating fudge."

It was too much for the both of us. We hooted and howled. I buried my head, but Miss Thomas saw me and banished me from the building. This much I knew: there would be no Christmas program for such a foolish child.

But Christmas is a time for grace, I had heard, and somehow my iniquities were forgotten in the joy of the season. Reserved for me was place in the choir, and I was even allowed to sing in the Christmas program. Squealing children and frantic parents electrified the church that Sunday evening. Roy Butler was there with two Chiquita Banana boxes, bursting forth with massive candy bags. Nuts. Hard candy. A mandarin orange, and soft candies if you dug deep and were real lucky.

Danny Brown was there, making faces at me from the balcony. I think Beth Freeman had even forgiven me. She recited from the Gospel of Luke, chapter two: "And the angel said unto them, 'Fear not: for, behold, I bring you good tidings of great joy…For unto you is born this day in the city of David a Saviour, which is Christ the Lord.'"

I'll never quite get over being forgiven at Christmastime.

And afterwards an amazing thing happened. Never in all my years do I recall seeing an extra candy bag, for Mr. Butler was meticulous. But this year there was. And that night Danny Brown left the church with his very own candy bag. You should have seen his eyes. It was a genuine Christmas miracle. Before he left, Danny smiled and slapped me between the shoulder blades, "Now we're on yonder star," he said.

It was a magical time.

It was Danny Brown's first Christmas.

"Christmas gives us an opportunity to pause and reflect on the important things around us."
-David Cameron

The Story of Christmas Reflection

Not everyone can sing. Some struggle to find any note, let alone the right note! Not everyone wants to sing. Heavy hearts can stifle a song. But when God wanted to announce the birth of His Son, He used an angelic choir. Startled shepherds dropped to the ground in fear when a heavenly host lit up the sky. They were assured by the shining figures that the song they brought was "good news" and "great joy." What they had to say was for "everybody!" The Christ has been born in Bethlehem. He is our Saviour who brings peace to people and glory to God.

Luke records the short lyric of this choir. Anyone could sing it in a few seconds. I doubt that angels came all this way for such a brief performance. I imagine that the song swelled like an unending round, until the shepherds themselves could join in. And they did. After they saw the Babe, they spread the song to everyone they saw! It was a song for those who can sing and those who can't. It was a song to lift the hearts of all people. It was a song that even Danny could sing. It was a song that is heard today, not just at Christmas, but continually in Heaven and on Earth.

Read the Reaction of the Shepherds in Luke 2:15-20

"When the angels had left them and gone into heaven, the shepherds said to one another, 'Let's go to Bethlehem and see this thing that has happened, which the Lord has told us about.'

So they hurried off and found Mary and Joseph, and the baby, who was lying in the manger. When they had seen him, they spread the word concerning what had been told them about this child, and all who heard it were amazed at what the shepherds said to them. But Mary treasured up all these things and pondered them in her heart. The shepherds returned, glorifying and praising God for all the things they had heard and seen, which were just as they had been told."

CHAPTER 5

A MARTHA STEWART CHRISTMAS

"Don't get me to wrap Christmas presents. It's not pretty. It's like watching a butcher wrap pork chops."
–Phil Callaway

D id you ever receive a Christmas letter from people who had the perfect year? A year in which their children excelled in school and were accepted at an Ivy League college by eighth grade? I thought of that when Martha Stewart sent me her Christmas letter via email on Christmas morning. Here it is.

Dear Phil,

This perfectly delightful note is being sent on paper I made myself so that I could tell you what I have been up to in early December. We had a delightful dusting of snow last night, so I got up early and made a sled out of old barn wood and leather straps and a glue gun. I hand-painted it in gold leaf, got out my loom, and wove a blanket in peaches and mauves to match. Now it's time to start making the placemats and napkins for thirty breakfast guests. I'm serving the old standard Stewart 12-course breakfast, but didn't have time to make the tables and chairs this morning, so I used the ones I already had. I did, however, take time to make the breakfast dishes. They're quite simple really. Just 100% Hungarian clay, which you can get at almost any Hungarian craft store. Well, I must run. I need to finish the buttonholes on the dress I'm wearing for breakfast. I'll get out the horse and sleigh and dash on over to the post office as soon as the glue dries on the envelope I'll be making. I hope the Laugh Again radio program is going well. You sure can be funny!

Love, Martha

Well, it hasn't been that kind of year at the Callaway house. Perhaps a return note to Martha would look something like this.

Dear Martha,

I'm writing this on the back of a recycled Christmas card from four years ago. Never mind the coffee stains on it and the green stuff. We have grandchildren now, so I have no idea what the green stuff is.

We tried decorating the tree to look like yours but our dog found it so realistic, that, well, we're returning to a fake tree next year. My wife says, "Hi!" She's trying to bake those little triple fudge cookies with the elves on them, but they keep coming out flat, like they got run over by a sleigh or something. She says the dough tastes better than the actual cookie anyway. So she's eating it now. With both hands.

Last night we tried those cute curly fries from your recipe book, but she burnt her arm on the curling iron, so that was that. I couldn't find the scissors to cut out snowflakes, so I used an old disposable razor. I likely should have covered the table with something, but it will be fine. We can sand and stain it next year.

Ramona tried your cranberry muffin recipe but our daughter was over and she likes to play pranks. I think she swapped the baking soda for baking powder. Thankfully, the dog liked them. My wife is on the phone with the vet now. As for me, I'd better figure out how to shut off the smoke alarm.

Merry Christmas,

Phil

I don't know about you, but a Martha Stewart Christmas won't be coming to our house anytime soon. Nothing seems picture perfect where we live. We thought the diaper stage was messy, but sometimes there are bigger messes when your kids get older. Life happens. Sadly, hardship takes no holidays. This year there were surgeries, calamities, and colonoscopies. Our grandbaby just fell down the stairs—all 14 of them (stairs, not babies). Thankfully, she got up, blinked, and screamed a little. In time, she was as good as new, but it meant another visit to a hospital that has stopped asking us for ID.

I find comfort in knowing that the first Christmas wasn't a Martha Stewart Christmas. That the greatest miracles always arise from the greatest messes. In January, Lord willing, we'll have two more grandbabies to love and pray for. How thankful I am that the same news that was heralded in ancient Palestine still rings through the crisp night air: "For unto us a child is born." In a world of biopsies and catastrophes, angiograms and mammograms, this truth will never change: Immanuel. God with us.

Now, I'm gonna join my wife and eat some cookie dough.

"He who has not Christmas in his heart will never find it under a tree."
-Roy L. Smith

The Story of Christmas Reflection

The "perfect" Christmas exists only in our imaginations. We conjure up idyllic images of gently falling snow, a pristine tree, and gifts that delight. But our real Christmas often has blizzards, trees that can't stand, and ugly sweaters. Even the very first Christmas was less than ideal.

Jesus' first bed was made of straw. The atmosphere was smelly at best. Mary and Joseph were far from home, and strange shepherds intruded into this private moment. Even the presents came late! So, was the first Christmas spoiled? God's Son came to Earth in humble circumstance, with little fanfare, ignored by most. But it was everything He intended it to be.

When we try to create Christmas with our own traditions and expectations, we will be disappointed. But if we welcome His Son to where we are, even Martha Stewart wouldn't be able to improve on it.

Read the story of Jesus' birth in Luke 2:1-7

"In those days Caesar Augustus issued a decree that a census should be taken of the entire Roman world. (This was the first census that took place while Quirinius was governor of Syria.) And everyone went to their own town to register.

So Joseph also went up from the town of Nazareth in Galilee to Judea, to Bethlehem the town of David, because he belonged to the house and line of David. He went there to register with Mary, who was pledged to be married to him and was expecting a child. While they were there, the time came for the baby to be born, and she gave birth to her firstborn, a son. She wrapped him in cloths and placed him in a manger, because there was no guest room available for them."

CHAPTER 6

A VERY DOGGIE CHRISTMAS

"Santa Claus had the right idea.
Visit people only once a year."
–Victor Borge

Christmas that year was cold. So cold that I did little else but stand and stare through the kitchen window, thinking, If I keep this up, maybe my wife will let me back into the house. I mentioned this to the family and everyone laughed. Even my wife.

The season had put us in a jolly mood, and knowing that our favourite Christmas guests were coming helped. Of all my friends, none was closer than Lauren, a TV news photo journalist, who was married to my wife's sister. A gentle giant, Lauren loved three things: God, his family, and a strong cup of coffee—one whiff of which was enough to keep me awake for days. When they finally pulled up, we were promptly introduced to the most recent addition to their family: a Border Collie named Kelly.

Now Border Collies are ranked number one in doggy intelligence, but let's face it, they still don't have a full deck. Acrobatic and pathologically energetic, a Border Collie locked indoors while the thermometer plunges will slowly and systematically lose its mind.

Needing something to herd, Kelly chose me.

Early the next morning, the Collie nosed our bedroom door open, chose my side of the bed, and stood sniffing, her face inches from mine. Before opening my eyes, I smelled Kelly's breath. The eagerness on her face said, "Cows! Get up!

They've broken through the fence again!"

I'm a night owl. I like to get up at the crack of noon. I said, "Get out of here or I'll call the pound."

She was undeterred. "Hey! It's six AM! Get up! Whatcha waitin' for? Let's go!"

I arrived at the breakfast table more bleary-eyed than usual, thanks to the fact that though I had locked Kelly out of our room, she sat outside torturing us by scratching the door every twelve seconds.

Lauren was in the kitchen pouring syrupy coffee into manly mugs. I told him about my wake-up call and he apologized. "No problem," I lied. But by the end of the day, it was a problem. Kelly followed me everywhere, engaged in frantic twirling, jumping and bouncing. The place was a mess. She chased whatever moved, brought toys, balls—even a plate for me to throw—then descended our stairs and chewed holes in every available ping pong ball.

Before bed, I threw Kelly a ball, then ran and locked myself in the bedroom. Twelve seconds passed. Then the soft scratching began.

My wife was standing in the bedroom. She was grinning. I was not. "That miserable dog is driving me crazy. Do you have some poison?"

Ramona's grin turned to a laugh. "Remember," she had the audacity to say, "Love me; love my dog."

And she was right. Life gets messy. With or without a dog. Particularly at Christmastime. Maybe that's why I have a little sticky note on my computer monitor: No one can drive you crazy unless you give them the keys. "Rejoice always," Paul said it much better in 1 Thessalonians 5:16. It's a short command, but it's enormously important. Rejoice when times are good? When dogs do things my way? No. "Rejoice in the Lord always." In the challenges and messes too. Nothing can pillage our peace unless we give it permission. Not even a dog.

I was a different boy when I left that room. Kelly could sense it. We took off down the stairs where I rounded up three tennis balls. We ran up and down the stairs ten times together. I panted heavily. She panted lightly.

Coffee has never been my cup of tea, but I said to Lauren, "Hit me with a cup of the strongest java you've got." I tossed it back and shuddered. Then we bundled up, pulled on our boots, and clumped outside where Kelly chased everything I could throw. She lost all three tennis balls in snowdrifts. "I'm so sorry," said Lauren. I laughed. "They're making more of them all the time. You can pick 'em up in stores."

We still talk about that Christmas. That night we crowded the table with family and friends. We played Dutch Blitz, sang Christmas carols, and ate sugar cookies, while a Border Collie named Kelly lay exhausted at our feet.

"Christmas is not as much about opening our presents as opening our hearts."
-Janice Maeditere

The Story of Christmas Reflection

Christmas does not always bring what you want. Gifts can be the wrong size or colour. Guests can be overwhelming and stay too long. Not everyone likes Christmas pudding. People don't want to be alone at Christmas, but some are. Christmas brings surprises, and not all of them are welcomed.

Joseph got the surprise of his life at Christmas. He was looking forward to his wedding with Mary, until she gave him stunning news. She was expecting a child but had done nothing improper. Joseph thought that was impossible. He wrestled with the right thing to do and decided to call off the wedding. The life he planned would not happen. Then a dream changed everything. God told him that Mary's child was the work of His Spirit. The child was to be named "Jesus" and He would save people from their sins. Joseph believed God and took Mary as his wife.

Joseph's life didn't go as he planned – but it went better! The Messiah would be raised under his roof. He would love the boy and teach Jesus how to be a carpenter. Joseph would be an instrument of God's plan. True, it took some getting used to, but he rejoiced in what God was doing. And as Phil learned when he had fun with a dog that wouldn't be ignored, things were better than he imagined.

Read Joseph's story in Matthew 1:20-23

"But after he had considered this, an angel of the Lord appeared to him in a dream and said, 'Joseph son of David, do not be afraid to take Mary home as your wife, because what is conceived in her is from the Holy Spirit. She will give birth to a son, and you are to give him the name Jesus, because he will save his people from their sins.' All this took place to fulfill what the Lord had said through the prophet: 'The virgin will conceive and give birth to a son, and they will call him Immanuel' (which means 'God with us')."

CHAPTER 7

CHRISTMAS AT CARNEGIE

"I once bought my kids a set of batteries for Christmas with a note on it saying, toys not included."
-Bernard Manning

When I was a kid, I didn't always want normal things on December 25th. Oh, I wanted ice skates and electric train sets and firecrackers, which my father never saw fit to bestow upon me. And one Christmas I wanted to be sick. I did. You see, people had not been all that charitable to me that year. My father had cut my hair so short that I needed a hat in July. A friend failed to acknowledge my birthday. My sister Ruth gave me a glass of apple juice. But it was from a pickle jar. I downed it in one gulp, and would surely have died, had God not had other plans for me.

And so it was that I noodled on a way to repay them. And finally it hit me: I would be sick. They would feel sorry for me then.

I didn't want to be badly sick. Not seriously ill. Just a broken leg perhaps. A minor bone. But it would swell up something fierce and cause doctors to whisper and confer and ponder if it wasn't more serious than they initially thought.

My sister would enter my room and sit on my bed and say, "How you doin' Phil? I'm so sorry for that pickle juice and for the time I told Mom what you said about me. Are you gonna be okay?" And I would respond in a weak little voice: "It won't be long now, I can see

angels. Take good care of the dog."

She would treat me so nicely then, and I would get all better on Christmas Eve—a Christmas miracle—and they would shower me with gifts.

As Christmas drew nigh, I awoke in my cold bed and allowed myself the illusion that I had been asked to sing a duet with Olivia Newton John, whom my brother had introduced me to in a rare moment of good taste. I imagined myself receiving her phone call wherein she says, in that lovely breathy tone, that she has heard of the loveliness of my voice when I use it in church and would I be interested in singing with her at Carnegie Hall during the International Festival of Christmas Festivities with a worldwide audience of 63 billion, and soon I am waking up at the Plaza Hotel to croissants and Coca cola—breakfast in a king-sized bed for which I can't quite find the edges.

Soon a call from the spacious lobby bids me ride in the limo to Carnegie where Miss John and I rehearse a medley of, "It Came Upon a Midnight Clear" and "I Honestly Love You." She cocks her head, turns to me as she reaches a high note, and lightly touches my arm, so caught up is she in the emotion of our duet. I am wearing red plaid flared pants and a green-striped turtleneck, and she compliments me on them both.

All good things must end, as did this dream. It is, after all, a long way from my home in Canada to New York City and singing with the most beautiful girl in Australia, but a boy wants what a boy wants and seldom is it something that will contribute to his moral well-being.

Sometimes the things we want so badly are smaller than we think in the grand scheme of things. But when we take time to examine the real reason we celebrate Christmas, we'll discover something vastly brighter and far more satisfying than anything a kid could dream up.

As with every other year, on radio, online, on TV, we're told that Christmas is all about us. One ad said, "All I want is something that will make my brother-in-law jealous." Small dreams, those.

When our son Jeffery was four, he woke each winter morning and made a beeline for the dress-up box at the end of the hall. He yanked on a Superman cape. He scrunched on a hat. Then he got down on all fours and chased his brother and sister throughout the house.

"I'm a kissing bull," he told them. They loved every terrifying minute of it.

One morning, Jeffrey charged into our bedroom and wrapped his mom in a hug. Looking up, he noticed tears streaming down her face. He couldn't know she had just received a shattering phone call from another sister who had Huntington's Disease. He couldn't know that his mama faced an uncertain future. But he began to sing the best news he'd ever heard: "I will not be afraid for God is with me." This he sang three times. An angel dressed up like a kissing bull.

"Love the giver more than the gift."
-Brigham Young

The Story of Christmas Reflection

Daydreams happen all year long, but they concentrate at Christmas. Adults and children flood their heads and hearts with their hopeful longings. Children become heroes and save the world. Adults get rich and explore the world. What they imagine shines brighter than what is really before them. But of course, eventually those daydreams fade.

The Christmas story is filled with dreams. God speaks to Joseph in a dream and rescues the family from Herod. Magi are warned by God in a dream. These dreams were not pretend. They were not "make believe." They were God's messages to be believed. Best of all – these dreams came true! Just as God told Joseph, Jesus was born as "Immanuel" – God is with us! He is with us when we're sick in bed. He is with us when bad news comes from the phone. He is with us through the loving hugs of family.

It's normal to daydream. But the plans and promises of God are better than any daydream we could come up with. Even if it is about singing a duet with Olivia Newton John.

Read about Joseph's dream in Matthew 2:13-15

"When they had gone, an angel of the Lord appeared to Joseph in a dream. 'Get up,' he said, 'take the child and his mother and escape to Egypt. Stay there until I tell you, for Herod is going to search for the child to kill him.' So he got up, took the child and his mother during the night and left for Egypt, where he stayed until the death of Herod. And so was fulfilled what the Lord had said through the prophet: 'Out of Egypt I called my son.'"

Let Phil tell the story!

Scan the QR code with your smart phone or tablet to go directly to a video of Phil Callaway sharing the story in this chapter. Watch with the whole family!

scan this code!

CHAPTER 8

THE MERCIFUL FIGHTER PILOT

"A lovely thing about Christmas is that it's compulsory, like a thunderstorm, and we all go through it together."
–Garrison Keillor

It's a holly jolly time, the Christmas season. That time of the year when complete grumps start to grin. People who look like bull dogs in November can transform into golden retrievers around December 15th. If you plan on cutting someone off in traffic this year, it's best to do it in mid-December. Chances are, the obstructed driver will wave with one of those "Don't worry, I've done less than admirable things myself" smiles on their face. Ah, Christmastime.

Not long ago, I read an unforgettable story of holiday kindness. Take a moment to pour yourself a hot drink, then I'd love to tell you about it.

It was December the 20th, 1943, five short days before Christmas. American Bomber Pilot Charlie Brown began his bombing run over Bremen, Germany in his B-17 Flying Fortress. But before the bomber could release its load, anti-aircraft flak shattered the Plexiglas nose, knocking out the number two engine and crippling engine number four. The bomber slowed to a dangerous crawl. Brown and his crew were forced to fall back, left vulnerable to sustained enemy attacks.

More than a dozen enemy fighters singled out the straggling B-17, attacking at will. Smoke curled from the number three engine. Bullets rendered the bomber's internal oxygen, hydraulic and electrical systems virtually useless. Worse, half of the bomber's rudder and its port elevator were lost. The tail gunner was slumped on his weapon, dead. Most of the crew were wounded. Lacking oxygen and hit in the right shoulder, Brown lost consciousness, then rallied in time to find the bomber in a dive. Somehow, he regained control and pulled her out of the steep plunge just in time, then began the impossible flight back to England.

The Germans on the ground spotted Brown's plane first, and ordered German fighter pilot ace Franz Stigler to finish it off. Franz took off in his Messerschmitt BF 109 and quickly caught up with the crippled plane.

Through the shattered bomber's airframe, Stigler could see the incapacitated crew. As he flew his fighter level with the bomber's cockpit, Brown thought, we're done for.

That's when it happened.

Franz Stigler waved at Charlie Brown.

If I can get them to divert to Sweden, thought Stigler, they will make it safely. He tried to communicate this to Charlie.

But the shocked pilot didn't understand and flew on. Stigler knew two things: The German anti-aircraft gunners would recognize a German plane and hold their fire. He also knew that protecting his enemy was a treasonous act, carrying with it the penalty of death. But for some reason, he didn't quit. Flying his Messerschmitt close to Brown's port side wing, he escorted the damaged B-17 over the coast until they reached open water. There Franz Stigler departed with a salute.

Before long, Brown and his battered crew landed safely in England.

In 1986, the retired Colonel Brown recalled his encounter with the kind German pilot who escorted him to safety, and wondered if there was some way he could track down the man to whom he owed his life. After more than four years of searching, Brown received a letter from Stigler, who was living in Canada. "I was the one," it said. Brown was ecstatic. Soon they spoke by phone. Stigler described his plane, the escort, the salute—everything Brown needed to know to confirm the identity of the German pilot who had spared his life.

Between 1990 and 2008, Charlie Brown and Franz Stigler became close friends and remained so until their deaths within several months of each other in 2008.

Hearing this, I was reminded of another story. You may have heard it before. It's the ultimate story of mercy, resulting in friendship. We celebrate each time we say the word Christmas. Each time we sing "Silent Night." Each time we crack open the book of Isaiah in the Bible and read the magnificent words, "Unto us a child is born, unto us a Son is given."

Mercy. We don't deserve it, but we can accept it. We can't earn it, but we can offer it. Each day may we bow down and give thanks that God has guided us into new life through faith in the one who has never left our side, Jesus Christ. His mercies are new with the morning light. After all He's done, let's spread some mercy around this Christmas.

"Even as an adult, I still find it hard to sleep on Christmas Eve."
-Carrie Latet

The Story of Christmas Reflection

There are more smiles at Christmas. Cheery greetings are exchanged between strangers. Cashiers get more conversations at the counter. People seem to be in a better mood – more connected with one another. That sense of "good will" has its roots in the very first Christmas.

When Zachariah burst into song at his son's birth, he said that God has fulfilled His promise to mankind, "that we should be saved from our enemies and from the hand of all that hate us." Our initial thought suggests that salvation from our enemies means we defeat them. But there is another way to win over enemies – that is, to make peace with them. Jesus came to Earth to offer peace to all who are hostile to God.

As Zachariah said, "…to give knowledge of salvation to His people in the forgiveness of their sins."

God makes peace with us. We can make peace with others. The story of Stigler and Brown demonstrates it. The friendliness of the season may fade by January, but the reconciliation of God in Jesus is an eternal grace.

 ## Read about Zachariah's Song in Luke 1:67-75

"His father Zechariah was filled with the Holy Spirit and prophesied:

'Praise be to the Lord, the God of Israel, because he has come to his people and redeemed them.

He has raised up a horn of salvation for us in the house of his servant David (as he said through his holy prophets of long ago), salvation from our enemies and from the hand of all who hate us—to show mercy to our ancestors and to remember his holy covenant, the oath he swore to our father Abraham: to rescue us from the hand of our enemies, and to enable us to serve him without fear in holiness and righteousness before him all our days.'"

CHAPTER 9

A BABY CHANGED EVERYTHING

"Christmas is a necessity. There has to be at least one day of the year to remind us that we're here for something else besides ourselves."
-Eric Sevareid

I was talking with a young guy a few weeks before Christmas. We were both in the toy aisle. He recognized me and wanted my advice. Sean had been married four years. A disagreement with his wife had clouded the Christmas season. I said, "This has been known to happen." He smiled. Marital discrepancies are no surprise to me, but the reason for his was.

"My wife wants children," he said, looking down at his socks. "I don't."

"Why?" I asked, thinking he was just like me at his age. You see, when I was first married, I didn't want to have children either. I found them completely disgusting. Christmas day was a reminder that children eat weird stuff. I watched my one-year-old nephew pick flies off the floor and pop them in his mouth. That's why if parents can't get their kids to eat stuff, they should just throw it on the floor. Then my nephew was off to slime doorknobs and get sticky junk on light switches. Kids are not the most sanitary objects you can bring into your home. So I understood this guy. But I asked him, "Why don't

you want children?" And this was his answer. "The world is a horrible place. Things have never been worse. There's terrorism. Disease. So much hatred. I can't imagine raising children in this culture."

What would you say to him? Maybe you'd agree. Maybe you'd say, "If you knew my family you'd understand why I don't want to pass along these genes." Maybe it's finances. The prospect of a lifetime of investing in children. And music lessons. Especially if they want to learn the tuba. Who needs that noise? And there's dealing with teachers. And making school lunches. And childbirth. If you're a woman, you say, "Who wants that kind of pain?" I don't blame you. It's bad enough for a man to be there and watch. Jeff Foxworthy said, "Watching a baby born is like watching a wet St. Bernard try to get through the cat door." Yup.

But let me ask you something. When did parents ever say, "You know, things are fantastic right now. This is the perfect time to have children"? When was it ever the ideal season to bring children into the world? Did folks in the Middle Ages who were moving rocks around say, "Don't the prospects look bright?" What about World War II? Or the Cold War, when we had the nuclear weaponry to destroy the world 63 times before breakfast? "Yahoo. Let's have kids." I don't think so.

It didn't look promising in first century Palestine either. Not from a human standpoint. Things were tough. The Romans had conquered. The timing seemed all wrong. But God knew the timing was just right. Galatians 4:4 says, "But when the time had fully come, God sent His Son, born of a woman…" He knew the time was right. People were longing for the Messiah's coming. There were no cell phones to distract people from the message. Seriously, God knew that false idols had failed to give the people victory over the Romans and they were searching. Greek philosophy had left many spiritually empty. Certain religions at that time emphasized a saviour-god and required worshipers to offer bloody sacrifices, perhaps making the message of a Saviour who would bring one ultimate sacrifice believable to them. A street form of the Greek language was spoken throughout the empire, so the gospel could be communicated to all. Rome had unified much of the world, so travel was now possible, allowing early Christians to spread the good news. The time was right for a child to change everything.

So what did I tell this guy? Just that our God is bigger. Trust Him. He's not worried. Not one little bit. I told him that the birth of my children changed my life for the good.

I think at its heart the reason Christmas stands above all other holidays for me is the promise it holds. In dark times a tiny baby was born to free us. And He's still freeing us today. I think of that as I hold my grandchild this Christmas. Maybe this guy will think of that next year when he holds his new baby. I hope they name him "Phil."

"The way you spend Christmas is far more important than how much."
-Henry David Thoreau

The Story of Christmas Reflection

Winter solstice is on December 21st. In the northern hemisphere, it is the shortest day of the year. It feels like the sun barely tips his hat to us and then disappears. It is fitting that Christmas occurs during the darkest days of the year. Our festive lights and candles proclaim throughout our homes and neighbourhoods that darkness does not have the final word.

When John's gospel speaks of the Christmas event, there is no mention of manger, star or magi. Instead John speaks about shadows and radiance. Jesus came into this dark world as Light. And as great as the darkness is in density and volume, Jesus shines truth and grace, giving light to all. The darkness of this Earth cannot extinguish the Light of Jesus. So, every generation, culture, place and people can have hope.

There is no pristine time to have a child. There is always darkness in this world. But that will change. Jesus didn't arrive on this Earth when everything was right. But this Child came to make everything right.

Read John's story of Jesus in John 1:1-9

"In the beginning was the Word, and the Word was with God, and the Word was God. He was with God in the beginning. Through him all things were made; without him nothing was made that has been made. In him was life, and that life was the light of all mankind. The light shines in the darkness, and the darkness has not overcome it.

There was a man sent from God whose name was John. He came as a witness to testify concerning that light, so that through him all might believe. He himself was not the light; he came only as a witness to the light.

The true light that gives light to everyone was coming into the world."

CHAPTER 10

YEAR WITHOUT A SUN

"If you believe that men and women are equal you have never watched me try to wrap a Christmas present."
–Phil Callaway

The moment you step off the train, you may think you're in a fairy tale. And you'll be close. The village of Obendorf, Austria, is quaint and spotless, its people friendly and approachable. The Salzach River wanders through this postcard hamlet framed by snow-covered Alps in the distance. A 10-minute stroll and you're climbing the steps to a small chapel on the site where a famous song was first performed. To your left, a hand-carved nativity stops you in your tracks and once inside the chapel, two stained glass windows honouring Father Joseph Mohr, the parish priest of St. Nicholas Church, will remind you why you came.

It was 1816 and the town was in crisis. Bargers made their living transporting salt down the river, but the river had flooded, putting many out of work. Twelve years of

Napoleonic wars had decimated the country. As Christmas approached, many were dubbing it, "The Year Without a Sun." Temperatures had nose-dived following a volcanic eruption in far away Indonesia, the largest in 1,300 years. The Northern Hemisphere was suffering an unprecedented global calamity as volcanic ash spewed skyward, circling the globe, eclipsing the sun, causing snow in summer, and triggering crop failure, poverty, starvation, and death. Many believed it to be the end of the world.

In the village of Mariapfarr, Father Joseph Mohr's congregation was poverty-stricken and in need of a fresh shot of hope. So, Mohr sat down and penned six poetic verses about the Christ child who had brought peace to this dark world—a Saviour who still saves, a God who still cares.

One year later, in 1817, Mohr transferred to the parish of St. Nicholas in the picturesque town of Oberndorf and, in time, took the poem he had written to his new friend, an esteemed local schoolteacher and organist Franz Gruber. "Would you compose the music for these six verses?" he asked. And so it was that a song was born. The two of them planned its debut after the Christmas Eve service was over, for in those days a guitar was seen as inappropriate for formal worship.

They had no idea if the song would be sung again. They couldn't know that the Strasser Family, popular folk singers throughout the Alps, would rehearse and sing it at festivals and fairs, while drumming up business for their parents who were makers of stylish winter gloves. They hadn't a clue that when those four Strasser kids harmonized, they would hit that song clean out of the park and all the way to the royal palace. That's right. Soon their presence would be requested by the king and queen, and those four nervous kids would give "Silent Night" a majestic performance and a royal nudge.

From there, the song would travel the globe, be translated into 300 languages, and bring hope and a badly-needed reminder that the Prince of Peace, the light of the world, had come.

When the Christmas Eve service ended in the parish of St. Nicholas, no one left the church. So the unlikely pair stood before the people and sang the words that would touch millions for centuries to come.

> "Silent night, holy night.
> All is calm, all is bright.
> Round yon virgin mother and child.
> Holy infant, so tender and mild.
> Sleep in heavenly peace, sleep in heavenly peace."

Some say the organ was broken that Christmas Eve, others say it was just fine. What we do know is that the spirits of the people were broken. And into that dark Christmas Eve, two friends, one a tenor, one a bass, brought "Silent Night" to life, with Mohr quietly strumming his sycamore wood guitar, a guitar you can view to this day in the Silent Night Museum in Hallein, Austria. Along with its sheet music, the guitar is insured for $1 million. Of course the message it helped bring is priceless.

We need it now as they needed it then: Christ the Saviour is born.

"It is Christmas in the heart that puts Christmas in the air."
-W.T. Ellis

The Story of Christmas Reflection

Every Christmas produces a fresh crop of Yuletide songs. The assumption seems to be that the music sung for years is getting old. Lyricists labour to create new verses that will capture our attention. Shopping malls vibrate with melodies about dancing around a Christmas tree, dreaming of a Christmas -white or blue, and mommy giving Santa a smooch. There's even a song that warns grandmas to beware of reindeer! Does the novel music improve the season? Maybe the older songs are better and the oldest one is best.

The first Christmas song was angelic. On the night of Jesus' birth, a heavenly host flooded the sky with light and sound. Their melody wasn't recorded but the words were. "Glory to God in the highest, and on earth peace among those with whom He is pleased!" These words have endured for more than two millennium. They've been echoed by countless cultures and language. They've been mimicked by Sunday School children with halos askew. They've been whispered as worship in prayerful tones. They are more than a song for the season; they are a promise for time and eternity. Mohr and Gruber would be stunned to see the reception of their "Silent Night." Repeatedly, it ranks as a Christmas favourite. They would also readily admit, the first one is better.

Read this first Christmas carol in Luke 2:11-14

"'Today in the town of David a Savior has been born to you; he is the Messiah, the Lord. This will be a sign to you: You will find a baby wrapped in cloths and lying in a manger.'

Suddenly a great company of the heavenly host appeared with the angel, praising God and saying,

'Glory to God in the highest heaven, and on earth peace to those on whom his favor rests.'"

CHAPTER 11

BEHIND THE SONGS

"There's nothing quite like the joy on a child's face Christmas morning when he pulls the wrapping off the iPad box you got him and finds out that it contains socks."
–Phil Callaway

Each year around about November 1st, we haul out the Christmas music and stream online, or listen to CDs, even vinyl records. Sometimes the stories behind the songs are as good as the songs themselves.

In July of 1945, Mel Torme dropped in on his friend Robert Wells to see how things were going. Wells was supposed to be writing songs for a couple of movies, but all he had written down were the words, "Chestnuts roasting...Jack Frost nipping... Yuletide carols... Folks dressed up like Eskimos." Mel Torme thought it was a great idea for a Christmas song, and he was right. Forty minutes later the song was finished. I always imagined those words were written near the North Pole by someone wrapped in a blankie sipping hot cocoa by the fire. But the song that we always called "Chipmunks Roasting on an Open Fire" was really "The Christmas Song." It was penned while World War II was ending, during a blistering California heat wave.

Originally sung by Bob Hope and Marilyn Maxwell, our next song was inspired by Salvation Army workers and their bells. When Ralph Blane mentioned the title "Tinkle Bells," to his wife, she laughed and informed him that "tinkle" was better known for something else. So he wisely changed it to "Have Yourself a Merry Little Tinkle." I'm kidding. "A Merry Little Christmas."

One of our most inspiring Christmas songs was written by the much-loved American poet Henry Wadsworth

Longfellow. In July of 1843, Henry married Fanny and before long they welcomed five children, though one passed away. In 1861 the opening shots of the American Civil War were fired, and on July 10, while cutting her daughter's hair, Fanny's

dress caught fire. Her husband desperately tried to extinguish the flames, first with a rug and then his own body. It was too late. His beloved bride Fanny died the next morning, and Henry Longfellow's burns were so severe that he couldn't attend his own wife's funeral. He would grow a beard to hide his disfigured face and at times feared he would be sent to an asylum on account of his grief.

During his first Christmas without Fanny, Longfellow wrote, "How inexpressibly sad are all holidays." And later, "I can make no record of these days. Better leave them wrapped in silence. Perhaps someday God will give me peace." The next Christmas he wrote, "'A merry Christmas' say the children, but that is no more for me."

As the Civil War divided the country, Longfellow's son Charles joined the army against his father's wishes and was critically wounded with a spinal injury. Christmas of 1863 is silent in Longfellow's journal. But the following Christmas day, three years after his wife's death, Longfellow listened as church bells announced the arrival of another painful Christmas. He took up a pen and wrote, "I heard the bells on Christmas day, their old familiar carols play, and wild and sweet the words repeat of peace on earth, good-will to men!"

But the song that began so pleasantly, took a dark turn. "And in despair I bowed my head; 'there is no peace on earth,' I said; 'for hate is strong, and mocks the song of peace on earth, good-will to men!'"

Then somehow from that dark Christmas, came the irrepressible triumph of hope: "Then pealed the bells more loud and deep: 'God is not dead, nor doth he sleep! The wrong shall fail, the right prevail, with peace on earth, good-will to men!'"

Longfellow's heartache continued. The Civil War raged on. Yet then, as today, Christmas came, and with it the reminder that amid hate and heartache, hope shines.

The times have been dark before. And into that darkness came the Light of the World. The Prince of Peace. A Saviour. Christ the Lord.

Our Messiah came into our mess with the promise that one day, He will make all things new. From our house to yours, a very merry Christmas.

"What is Christmas? It is tenderness for the past, courage for the present, hope for the future."
– Agnes M. Pahro

31

The Story of Christmas Reflection

Christmas is filled with singing. You probably have your favourite carol or seasonal song. Singing is not something we impose upon Christmas, but singing is embedded in the narrative. The Christmas story has four songs and they each have a name. Mary sings the Magnificat (Luke 1:46-55). Zachariah's song is called the Benedictus (Luke 1:68-79). The angelic choir recited the Gloria (Luke 2:14) and Simeon whispers Nunc Dimittis (Luke 2:29-32).

The Latin names for the songs may confuse us but they all have a simple theme. Mary "magnifies" God with praise. Zachariah speaks of God's "blessing" to all. The angels proclaim "glory" to God. Simeon sings that he can "now depart" from this life, having seen the Messiah. Their songs are different but their cause is the same. God is the reason for the songs. He has done great things. He has blessed us with Jesus as the sunrise to our darkness. He gave the world good news and great joy. He has prepared salvation for us all.

So, sing this Christmas! Add your voice to the assembly of saints in Heaven and on Earth. Sing off key if you must. Sing loudly to be heard. Sing from the depths of your joy. And whatever you sing, let God be the reason for your song.

Read the song of Mary in Luke 1:46-55

"And Mary said: 'My soul glorifies the Lord and my spirit rejoices in God my Savior, for he has been mindful of the humble state of his servant. From now on all generations will call me blessed, for the Mighty One has done great things for me—holy is his name. His mercy extends to those who fear him, from generation to generation. He has performed mighty deeds with his arm; he has scattered those who are proud in their inmost thoughts. He has brought down rulers from their thrones but has lifted up the humble. He has filled the hungry with good things but has sent the rich away empty. He has helped his servant Israel, remembering to be merciful to Abraham and his descendants forever, just as he promised our ancestors.'"

Let Phil tell the story!

Scan the QR code with your smart phone or tablet to go directly to a video of Phil Callaway sharing the story in this chapter. Watch with the whole family!

scan this code!

CHAPTER 12

SWEET POTATOES

*"You can tell a lot about a person by the way they
handle three things: lost luggage, a January blizzard,
and tangled Christmas lights."*
–Maya Angelou

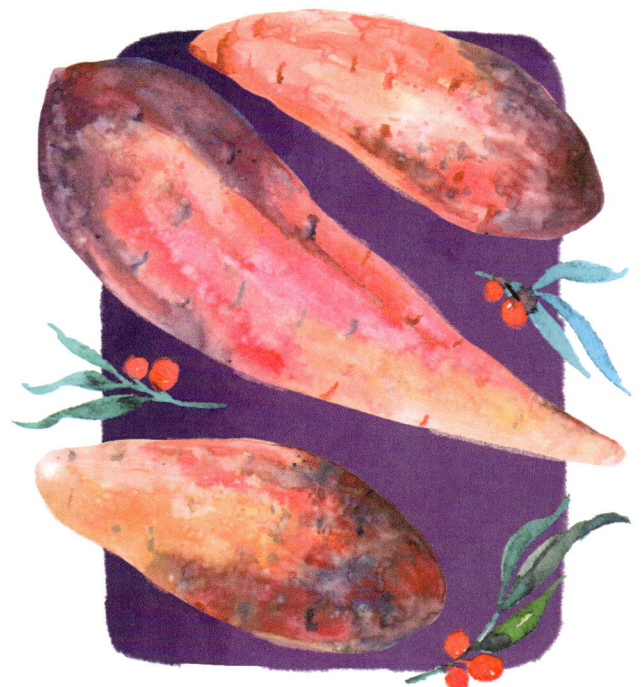

I have two simple New Year's resolutions this year. I resolve to think twice before pushing "reply all" in response to emails. And I plan on lifting the barbeque lid before lighting the barbeque—that way I will have my eyebrows all year long.

It's been quite a year at the Callaway house. We've doubled the number of grandchildren with the promise of more arriving soon. I don't think I've ever felt the need to pray like I have lately. Seriously. What if these grandkids turn out like me? I thought my name was Cut It Out when I was a kid. How about you? Do you find yourself saying, "If God doesn't show up, I'm toast?" When we face a new year, worry and anxiety can move to the surface faster than a toupee in a windstorm. Does God answer prayer? Does He even care about the small things?

It was New Year's Eve. The director of a New York food bank picked up the phone. An old woman had called. "I've always loved the annual New Year's dinner at the food bank," she said, "but I'm too sick to go anywhere this year. I'm alone. I have no money, and no one to pick anything up for me. It's too much to ask, but could someone bring me some food?"

The food bank director found herself saying, "Yes. In fact, I'll bring New Year's dinner to you myself." The old woman thanked the director, then said, "Will there be any sweet potatoes on the menu?" "No," answered the director.

"We depend on donated food. No sweet potatoes have been donated." "That's fine," the old woman said, laughing. "When I was a little girl we always had sweet potatoes at New Year's. It's been a tradition throughout my life. I had a bit of a craving, I guess." Then she laughed again. "I'll pray that the food bank receives a donation of sweet potatoes."

The director smiled and hung up the phone. She decided to get in her car, drive to the grocery store, and buy that sweet woman a sweet potato. She would cook it and bring it along with dinner. But reaching the parking lot, she found that her car was blocked by a large delivery truck. Irritated, she said to the driver, "You can't park here. I need to move my car."

The driver said, "I'm so sorry. I haven't been to the food bank before. I didn't know where to park. I have a load of… sweet potatoes."

The director of the food bank leaned forward. "You what?"

"Well," the driver apologized, "they're just small and knobby. The grocery stores don't want 'em. Customers prefer

The grocery stores don't want 'em. Customers prefer big, plump sweet potatoes. We thought you could use them."

The food bank director's grin was as wide as her eyes. "How many do you have?" she asked.

The driver apologized again, "Only about a hundred bushels. Is that enough?"

Well, the director couldn't get back to her office fast enough. She was laughing when she called the old woman. "I have great news," she said. "Someone brought sweet potatoes. We have more than we can possibly cook. Please, do me a favour. Stop praying!" The two laughed together. Then the old woman said, "I sure hope they're the small kind. I've never liked those big, plump ones."

Now, I'm not guaranteeing sweet potatoes. But God listens to those He loves. He knows our every need. He is worthy of our trust. Let's bring our concerns to Him every day this year.

Philippians 4:6-7 in The Message has been such a great reminder when I lie awake wondering about what's ahead.

"Don't fret or worry. Instead of worrying, pray. Let petitions and praises shape your worries into prayers, letting God know your concerns. Before you know it, a sense of God's wholeness, everything coming together for good, will come and settle you down."

I wish for you that level of joy and peace in the New Year. May He supply all your "sweet potato" needs.

Immanuel. God is with you, my friend.

~~~~~~~~~~~

"One of the most glorious messes in the world is the mess created in the living room on Christmas Day."
-Andy Rooney

The Story of Christmas Reflection

What if everyone got what they needed this Christmas? What would be under the tree? There would be the usual assortment of toys, clothes, gadgets and books. But, with very few exceptions, these are not what we need. We need a cure for cancer. We need global hostilities to end. We need hospitals to be empty and everyone to have a home. We need the hug of loved ones, perhaps distant, perhaps deceased. We need our wounded hearts to be healed. We need healthy minds and whole bodies. We need safe streets and strong communities. We need our own wrongs to be amended. We need our sins to be forgiven. We need all this and so much more.

But these things won't be under the tree. In fact, looking there is useless. It's not that people aren't trying to do these things, it's just that they are beyond anyone's ability. We can't save ourselves, we need to be saved. The truth of Christmas is this. God has given to us what we need. We need Jesus. From Him and for Him all our needs will be resolved. Eternity is a time and place when all our wants will be met and our needs will be no more. Even better than sweet potatoes! It will feel like Christmas forever, because we will be with Christ forever— our hopes realized, our dreams fulfilled, our joy complete.

Read the prophetic promise of
Jesus in Isaiah 9:6-7

"For to us a child is born, to us a son is given, and the government will be on his shoulders. And he will be called Wonderful Counselor, Mighty God, Everlasting Father, Prince of Peace. Of the greatness of his government and peace there will be no end. He will reign on David's throne and over his kingdom, establishing and upholding it with justice and righteousness from that time on and forever. The zeal of the Lord Almighty will accomplish this."

www.ingramcontent.com/pod-product-compliance
Lightning Source LLC
Chambersburg PA
CBRC090842120626
46551CB00008B/735